50 Appetizers for Dinner Parties Recipes

By: Kelly Johnson

Table of Contents

- Roasted Chickpeas
- Thai Spring Rolls
- Stuffed Peppers with Cheese
- Tandoori Chicken Skewers
- Marinated Olives
- Caramelized Onion Tartlets
- Chicken Wings with Various Sauces
- Eggplant Dip with Pita
- Brie and Cranberry Tart
- Shrimp and Grits Bites
- Parmesan Crisps with Dip
- Stuffed Mini Peppers
- Caviar on Blinis
- Feta and Spinach Stuffed Pastries
- Garlic Parmesan Cauliflower Bites

Stuffed Mushrooms

Ingredients:

- 1 lb large mushrooms, stems removed
- 1 cup cream cheese, softened
- 1/2 cup grated Parmesan cheese
- 1/4 cup breadcrumbs
- 2 cloves garlic, minced
- 2 tbsp fresh parsley, chopped
- Salt and pepper to taste

Instructions:

Preheat the oven to 375°F (190°C). In a bowl, mix cream cheese, Parmesan, breadcrumbs, garlic, parsley, salt, and pepper until well combined. Stuff each mushroom cap with the mixture and place them on a baking sheet. Bake for 20-25 minutes until the mushrooms are tender and the tops are golden. Serve warm.

Caprese Skewers

Ingredients:

- 1 pint cherry tomatoes
- 8 oz fresh mozzarella balls
- Fresh basil leaves
- Balsamic glaze
- Salt and pepper to taste
- Skewers or toothpicks

Instructions:

On each skewer, thread a cherry tomato, a basil leaf, and a mozzarella ball. Repeat until the skewer is filled. Drizzle with balsamic glaze and sprinkle with salt and pepper before serving.

Spinach and Artichoke Dip

Ingredients:

- 1 cup frozen spinach, thawed and drained
- 1 cup canned artichoke hearts, chopped
- 1 cup cream cheese, softened
- 1/2 cup sour cream
- 1/2 cup grated Parmesan cheese
- 1 cup shredded mozzarella cheese
- 2 cloves garlic, minced
- Salt and pepper to taste

Instructions:

Preheat the oven to 350°F (175°C). In a mixing bowl, combine spinach, artichokes, cream cheese, sour cream, Parmesan, mozzarella, garlic, salt, and pepper. Spread the mixture into a baking dish and bake for 25-30 minutes until bubbly and golden. Serve with tortilla chips or bread.

Bacon-Wrapped Dates

Ingredients:

- 1 lb pitted dates
- 8 oz bacon, cut in half
- Toothpicks

Instructions:

Preheat the oven to 400°F (200°C). Wrap each date with a half slice of bacon and secure with a toothpick. Place on a baking sheet and bake for 15-20 minutes until the bacon is crispy. Serve warm.

Bruschetta with Tomato and Basil

Ingredients:

- 1 French baguette, sliced
- 2 cups diced tomatoes
- 1/4 cup fresh basil, chopped
- 2 cloves garlic, minced
- 2 tbsp olive oil
- Salt and pepper to taste

Instructions:

Preheat the oven to 400°F (200°C). In a bowl, combine tomatoes, basil, garlic, olive oil, salt, and pepper. Place baguette slices on a baking sheet and toast for about 5 minutes. Top each slice with the tomato mixture and serve.

Deviled Eggs

Ingredients:

- 6 large eggs, hard-boiled and peeled
- 3 tbsp mayonnaise
- 1 tsp Dijon mustard
- 1/2 tsp paprika
- Salt and pepper to taste
- Fresh chives for garnish

Instructions:

Cut the hard-boiled eggs in half and remove the yolks. In a bowl, mash the yolks with mayonnaise, mustard, paprika, salt, and pepper. Spoon or pipe the mixture back into the egg whites. Garnish with chopped chives before serving.

Mini Quiches

Ingredients:

- 1 cup milk
- 4 large eggs
- 1 cup shredded cheese (e.g., cheddar)
- 1/2 cup diced vegetables (e.g., bell peppers, onions)
- Salt and pepper to taste
- Pre-made pastry shells or phyllo dough

Instructions:

Preheat the oven to 375°F (190°C). In a mixing bowl, whisk together milk, eggs, salt, and pepper. Place pastry shells on a baking sheet. Fill each shell with cheese, vegetables, and pour the egg mixture on top until filled. Bake for 20-25 minutes until set and golden. Serve warm.

Shrimp Cocktail

Ingredients:

- 1 lb cooked shrimp, peeled and deveined
- 1 cup cocktail sauce
- Lemon wedges for serving

Instructions:

Arrange the shrimp on a platter and serve with cocktail sauce and lemon wedges on the side for dipping.

Meatballs in Marinara

Ingredients:

- 1 lb ground beef or turkey
- 1/2 cup breadcrumbs
- 1/4 cup grated Parmesan cheese
- 1 egg
- 2 cloves garlic, minced
- 1 tsp Italian seasoning
- Salt and pepper to taste
- 2 cups marinara sauce

Instructions:

Preheat the oven to 400°F (200°C). In a bowl, combine ground meat, breadcrumbs, Parmesan, egg, garlic, Italian seasoning, salt, and pepper. Form mixture into meatballs and place on a baking sheet. Bake for 20-25 minutes until cooked through. In a saucepan, heat marinara sauce and add baked meatballs. Simmer for 5-10 minutes and serve.

Cheese and Charcuterie Board

Ingredients:

- Assorted cheeses (e.g., brie, cheddar, gouda)
- Assorted cured meats (e.g., salami, prosciutto)
- Crackers or bread
- Fresh fruits (e.g., grapes, figs)
- Nuts (e.g., almonds, walnuts)
- Honey or jam for drizzling

Instructions:

Arrange the cheeses, cured meats, crackers, fresh fruits, and nuts on a large board or platter. Add small bowls of honey or jam. Serve with cheese knives and toothpicks for easy serving.

Vegetable Spring Rolls

Ingredients:

- 8 rice paper wrappers
- 1 cup shredded carrots
- 1 cup sliced bell peppers
- 1 cup cucumber, julienned
- Fresh herbs (e.g., mint, cilantro)
- Soy sauce or peanut sauce for dipping

Instructions:

Fill a shallow bowl with warm water. Dip one rice paper wrapper into the water for a few seconds until softened, then lay it flat. Add a small amount of each vegetable and herbs to the center. Fold the sides over and roll tightly. Repeat with remaining wrappers. Serve with soy sauce or peanut sauce.

Hummus and Pita Chips

Ingredients:

- 1 can chickpeas, drained and rinsed
- 1/4 cup tahini
- 2 tbsp olive oil
- 2 tbsp lemon juice
- 1 clove garlic, minced
- Salt to taste
- Pita bread, cut into triangles

Instructions:

In a food processor, blend chickpeas, tahini, olive oil, lemon juice, garlic, and salt until smooth. Adjust seasoning to taste. For pita chips, preheat the oven to 350°F (175°C), brush pita triangles with olive oil, and bake for 10-12 minutes until crispy. Serve hummus with pita chips.

Antipasto Skewers

Ingredients:

- 1 cup cherry tomatoes
- 1 cup mozzarella balls
- 1 cup sliced salami or pepperoni
- 1/2 cup olives (green or black)
- Fresh basil leaves
- Skewers or toothpicks

Instructions:

On each skewer, thread a cherry tomato, mozzarella ball, a slice of salami, an olive, and a basil leaf. Repeat until the skewer is filled. Serve as a refreshing appetizer.

Chicken Satay with Peanut Sauce

Ingredients:

- 1 lb chicken breast, sliced into strips
- 1/4 cup soy sauce
- 1 tbsp honey
- 1 tbsp vegetable oil
- 1 tsp ground cumin
- Skewers

Instructions:

In a bowl, mix soy sauce, honey, oil, and cumin. Marinate chicken strips in the mixture for at least 30 minutes. Thread chicken onto skewers and grill or cook in a skillet over medium heat for 5-7 minutes until cooked through. Serve with peanut sauce.

Guacamole and Tortilla Chips

Ingredients:

- 2 ripe avocados
- 1 lime, juiced
- 1/2 cup diced tomatoes
- 1/4 cup diced onion
- 1 clove garlic, minced
- Salt to taste
- Tortilla chips for serving

Instructions:

In a bowl, mash avocados with lime juice. Stir in tomatoes, onion, garlic, and salt. Adjust seasoning to taste. Serve with tortilla chips for dipping.

Roasted Red Pepper and Feta Dip

Ingredients:

- 1 cup roasted red peppers, drained
- 1 cup feta cheese, crumbled
- 1/4 cup Greek yogurt
- 1 clove garlic, minced
- 1 tbsp olive oil
- Salt and pepper to taste

Instructions:

In a food processor, combine roasted red peppers, feta cheese, Greek yogurt, garlic, olive oil, salt, and pepper. Blend until smooth. Serve with pita bread or crackers.

Crispy Fried Calamari

Ingredients:

- 1 lb calamari, cleaned and sliced into rings
- 1 cup buttermilk
- 1 cup all-purpose flour
- 1/2 cup cornmeal
- Salt and pepper to taste
- Vegetable oil for frying
- Lemon wedges for serving

Instructions:

Soak the calamari rings in buttermilk for at least 30 minutes. In a bowl, mix flour, cornmeal, salt, and pepper. Heat oil in a deep pan over medium-high heat. Dredge the soaked calamari in the flour mixture and fry in batches until golden brown, about 2-3 minutes. Drain on paper towels and serve with lemon wedges.

Pigs in a Blanket

Ingredients:

- 1 package crescent roll dough
- 1 package mini hot dogs
- 1 egg, beaten (for egg wash)
- Mustard or ketchup for dipping

Instructions:

Preheat the oven to 375°F (190°C). Unroll the crescent roll dough and cut it into triangles. Place a mini hot dog on the wider end of each triangle and roll it up. Place on a baking sheet, brush with beaten egg, and bake for 12-15 minutes until golden. Serve with mustard or ketchup.

Smoked Salmon Canapés

Ingredients:

- 1 baguette, sliced into thin rounds
- 4 oz cream cheese, softened
- 4 oz smoked salmon
- Fresh dill for garnish
- Capers for garnish

Instructions:

Toast the baguette slices in the oven until lightly golden. Spread cream cheese on each slice, top with smoked salmon, and garnish with dill and capers. Arrange on a platter and serve.

Mini Tacos

Ingredients:

- 1 lb ground beef or turkey
- 1 taco seasoning packet
- 12 mini tortillas
- Shredded lettuce, diced tomatoes, shredded cheese, and salsa for toppings

Instructions:

In a skillet, cook the ground meat over medium heat until browned. Drain excess fat and stir in taco seasoning according to package instructions. Warm the mini tortillas and fill each with the seasoned meat. Top with lettuce, tomatoes, cheese, and salsa.

Spinach Feta Phyllo Puffs

Ingredients:

- 1 package phyllo dough, thawed
- 2 cups fresh spinach, chopped
- 1 cup feta cheese, crumbled
- 1/4 cup cream cheese, softened
- 1 egg, beaten (for egg wash)
- Olive oil for brushing

Instructions:

Preheat the oven to 375°F (190°C). In a bowl, mix spinach, feta, cream cheese, and half of the beaten egg. Cut phyllo dough into squares and layer a few sheets, brushing each with olive oil. Place a spoonful of the spinach mixture in the center and fold into a triangle. Brush the tops with egg wash and bake for 20-25 minutes until golden.

Olive Tapenade on Crostini

Ingredients:

- 1 cup mixed olives, pitted
- 2 tbsp capers
- 1 clove garlic
- 2 tbsp olive oil
- 1 French baguette, sliced
- Fresh parsley for garnish

Instructions:

In a food processor, blend olives, capers, garlic, and olive oil until chunky. Toast baguette slices until golden. Spread olive tapenade on each crostini and garnish with parsley.

Coconut Shrimp

Ingredients:

- 1 lb large shrimp, peeled and deveined
- 1 cup shredded coconut
- 1/2 cup breadcrumbs
- 1/4 cup flour
- 2 eggs, beaten
- Salt and pepper to taste
- Vegetable oil for frying

Instructions:

In a bowl, mix coconut, breadcrumbs, salt, and pepper. Dredge shrimp in flour, dip in beaten eggs, and coat with the coconut mixture. Heat oil in a pan over medium heat and fry the shrimp until golden, about 3-4 minutes per side. Drain on paper towels and serve.

Sweet Potato Bites with Avocado

Ingredients:

- 2 medium sweet potatoes, sliced into rounds
- 1 avocado, mashed
- Lime juice to taste
- Salt and pepper to taste
- Fresh cilantro for garnish

Instructions:

Preheat the oven to 400°F (200°C). Arrange sweet potato rounds on a baking sheet and brush with olive oil. Roast for 25-30 minutes until tender. In a bowl, mix mashed avocado with lime juice, salt, and pepper. Top each sweet potato round with the avocado mixture and garnish with cilantro before serving.

Mini Sliders

Ingredients:

- 1 lb ground beef
- 1/2 cup breadcrumbs
- 1 egg
- 1 tsp garlic powder
- Salt and pepper to taste
- Slider buns
- Cheese slices (optional)
- Lettuce, tomato, and condiments for serving

Instructions:

Preheat the grill or a skillet over medium heat. In a bowl, mix ground beef, breadcrumbs, egg, garlic powder, salt, and pepper. Form into small patties and cook for 3-4 minutes on each side. If using cheese, place a slice on each patty during the last minute of cooking to melt. Assemble sliders on buns with lettuce, tomato, and condiments.

Tomato Basil Soup Shots

Ingredients:

- 2 cans (14 oz each) diced tomatoes
- 1 cup vegetable broth
- 1/2 cup heavy cream
- 1/4 cup fresh basil, chopped
- Salt and pepper to taste
- Olive oil for drizzling

Instructions:

In a pot, combine diced tomatoes and vegetable broth. Bring to a simmer for 10 minutes. Blend the mixture until smooth, then stir in heavy cream and basil. Season with salt and pepper. Serve in small shot glasses and drizzle with olive oil.

Korean BBQ Meatballs

Ingredients:

- 1 lb ground beef or pork
- 1/4 cup breadcrumbs
- 1/4 cup green onions, chopped
- 1 tbsp soy sauce
- 1 tbsp sesame oil
- 1 tbsp ginger, minced
- 1 tbsp garlic, minced
- Sesame seeds for garnish

Instructions:

Preheat the oven to 400°F (200°C). In a bowl, mix ground meat, breadcrumbs, green onions, soy sauce, sesame oil, ginger, and garlic. Form into small meatballs and place on a baking sheet. Bake for 15-20 minutes until cooked through. Garnish with sesame seeds before serving.

Zucchini Fritters

Ingredients:

- 2 medium zucchinis, grated
- 1/2 cup flour
- 1/4 cup grated Parmesan cheese
- 1 egg
- Salt and pepper to taste
- Olive oil for frying

Instructions:

In a bowl, squeeze out excess moisture from grated zucchini. Mix zucchini, flour, Parmesan, egg, salt, and pepper. Heat olive oil in a skillet over medium heat. Drop spoonfuls of the mixture into the skillet and flatten slightly. Fry for 3-4 minutes on each side until golden brown. Drain on paper towels before serving.

Baked Brie with Jam

Ingredients:

- 1 round of Brie cheese
- 1/4 cup fruit jam (such as raspberry or apricot)
- 1 sheet puff pastry, thawed
- 1 egg, beaten (for egg wash)
- Crackers or sliced baguette for serving

Instructions:

Preheat the oven to 375°F (190°C). Roll out puff pastry and place the Brie in the center. Spread jam on top of the Brie and fold the pastry over the cheese, sealing the edges. Brush with beaten egg and bake for 20-25 minutes until golden. Serve warm with crackers or baguette.

Cucumber Bites with Cream Cheese

Ingredients:

- 1 large cucumber, sliced into rounds
- 4 oz cream cheese, softened
- 1 tbsp fresh dill, chopped
- Salt and pepper to taste

Instructions:

In a bowl, mix cream cheese, dill, salt, and pepper until well combined. Spread a small amount of the cream cheese mixture on each cucumber slice. Arrange on a platter and serve.

Crab Cakes with Remoulade

Ingredients:

- 1 lb crab meat
- 1/2 cup breadcrumbs
- 1/4 cup mayonnaise
- 1 egg
- 1 tbsp Dijon mustard
- 1 tbsp Worcestershire sauce
- Salt and pepper to taste
- Oil for frying
- 1/2 cup mayonnaise (for remoulade)
- 1 tbsp capers, chopped
- 1 tbsp fresh parsley, chopped

Instructions:

In a bowl, mix crab meat, breadcrumbs, mayonnaise, egg, Dijon mustard, Worcestershire sauce, salt, and pepper. Form into small patties. Heat oil in a skillet over medium heat and fry the crab cakes for 4-5 minutes on each side until golden. For the remoulade, mix mayonnaise with capers and parsley. Serve crab cakes with remoulade on the side.

Caprese Salad Bites

Ingredients:

- Cherry tomatoes, halved
- Fresh mozzarella balls
- Fresh basil leaves
- Balsamic glaze for drizzling
- Salt and pepper to taste

Instructions:

On small skewers or toothpicks, thread a cherry tomato half, a basil leaf, and a mozzarella ball. Repeat until all ingredients are used. Drizzle with balsamic glaze and sprinkle with salt and pepper before serving.

Baked Potato Skins

Ingredients:

- 4 large russet potatoes
- 1 cup shredded cheddar cheese
- 1/2 cup cooked bacon, crumbled
- 1/4 cup sour cream
- 2 green onions, chopped
- Olive oil
- Salt and pepper to taste

Instructions:

Preheat the oven to 400°F (200°C). Bake potatoes for 45-60 minutes until tender. Let cool, then cut in half and scoop out some flesh, leaving a thin layer. Brush potato skins with olive oil, season with salt and pepper, and bake for an additional 10 minutes. Fill each skin with cheese and bacon, return to the oven until cheese melts, then top with sour cream and green onions before serving.

Asparagus Wrapped in Prosciutto

Ingredients:

- 1 lb asparagus, trimmed
- 8 oz prosciutto, thinly sliced
- Olive oil
- Salt and pepper to taste
- Lemon wedges for serving

Instructions:

Preheat the oven to 400°F (200°C). Wrap a slice of prosciutto around each asparagus spear. Place on a baking sheet and drizzle with olive oil, then season with salt and pepper. Bake for 15-20 minutes until the asparagus is tender and the prosciutto is crispy. Serve with lemon wedges.

Falafel with Tahini Sauce

Ingredients:

- 1 can (15 oz) chickpeas, drained and rinsed
- 1/4 cup fresh parsley, chopped
- 1/4 cup onion, chopped
- 2 cloves garlic, minced
- 1 tsp cumin
- 1 tsp coriander
- 1/4 cup flour
- Salt and pepper to taste
- Oil for frying
- 1/4 cup tahini
- 1 tbsp lemon juice
- Water to thin

Instructions:

In a food processor, combine chickpeas, parsley, onion, garlic, cumin, coriander, flour, salt, and pepper. Pulse until a coarse mixture forms. Form into small balls. Heat oil in a skillet over medium heat and fry the falafel for 3-4 minutes on each side until golden brown. For the tahini sauce, mix tahini, lemon juice, and water until smooth. Serve falafel with tahini sauce.

Roasted Chickpeas

Ingredients:

- 1 can (15 oz) chickpeas, drained and rinsed
- 1 tbsp olive oil
- 1 tsp smoked paprika
- 1/2 tsp garlic powder
- Salt to taste

Instructions:

Preheat the oven to 400°F (200°C). Pat chickpeas dry with a paper towel and toss with olive oil, smoked paprika, garlic powder, and salt. Spread on a baking sheet and roast for 20-30 minutes until crispy, shaking the pan halfway through. Let cool before serving.

Thai Spring Rolls

Ingredients:

- 8 rice paper wrappers
- 1 cup cooked shrimp or chicken, sliced
- 1 cup lettuce, shredded
- 1/2 cup carrots, julienned
- 1/2 cup cucumber, julienned
- Fresh herbs (mint, cilantro)
- Peanut sauce or sweet chili sauce for dipping

Instructions:

Fill a shallow dish with warm water. Soak one rice paper wrapper for about 10 seconds until soft. Lay it flat on a clean surface and layer shrimp or chicken, lettuce, carrots, cucumber, and herbs in the center. Fold the sides over and roll tightly. Repeat with remaining ingredients. Serve with peanut sauce or sweet chili sauce.

Stuffed Peppers with Cheese

Ingredients:

- 4 bell peppers, halved and seeded
- 1 cup cooked rice
- 1 cup black beans, drained
- 1 cup corn
- 1 cup shredded cheese (cheddar or mozzarella)
- 1 tsp cumin
- Salt and pepper to taste
- 1/4 cup salsa

Instructions:

Preheat the oven to 375°F (190°C). In a bowl, mix cooked rice, black beans, corn, half of the cheese, cumin, salt, pepper, and salsa. Stuff the pepper halves with the mixture and place them in a baking dish. Top with remaining cheese. Cover with foil and bake for 30 minutes. Remove foil and bake for an additional 10 minutes until the cheese is bubbly.

Tandoori Chicken Skewers

Ingredients:

- 1 lb chicken breast, cubed
- 1/2 cup yogurt
- 2 tbsp tandoori spice mix
- 1 tbsp lemon juice
- Salt to taste
- Skewers (soaked in water if wooden)

Instructions:

In a bowl, combine yogurt, tandoori spice mix, lemon juice, and salt. Add chicken cubes and marinate for at least 1 hour. Preheat the grill or oven to medium-high heat. Thread marinated chicken onto skewers and grill for 10-15 minutes, turning occasionally, until cooked through. Serve with dipping sauce.

Marinated Olives

Ingredients:

- 1 cup mixed olives (green and black)
- 2 tbsp olive oil
- 1 tsp dried oregano
- 1 clove garlic, minced
- Zest of 1 lemon
- Crushed red pepper flakes (optional)

Instructions:

In a bowl, combine olives, olive oil, oregano, garlic, lemon zest, and red pepper flakes if using. Toss to coat and let marinate for at least 30 minutes before serving.

Caramelized Onion Tartlets

Ingredients:

- 1 sheet puff pastry, thawed
- 2 large onions, thinly sliced
- 2 tbsp butter
- 1 tbsp olive oil
- 1/2 cup goat cheese or feta cheese, crumbled
- Fresh thyme for garnish
- Salt and pepper to taste

Instructions:

Preheat the oven to 400°F (200°C). In a skillet, heat butter and olive oil over medium heat. Add onions and cook, stirring occasionally, for about 20-25 minutes until caramelized. Roll out the puff pastry and cut into squares. Place on a baking sheet and top each square with caramelized onions and cheese. Bake for 15-20 minutes until golden brown. Garnish with fresh thyme before serving.

Chicken Wings with Various Sauces

Ingredients:

- 2 lbs chicken wings
- Salt and pepper to taste
- 1 tbsp olive oil
- 1 cup buffalo sauce (or any sauce of choice)
- Optional: barbecue sauce, honey garlic sauce, or teriyaki sauce

Instructions:

Preheat the oven to 400°F (200°C). Toss the chicken wings with olive oil, salt, and pepper. Arrange on a baking sheet in a single layer. Bake for 40-45 minutes, flipping halfway through, until crispy. Toss the baked wings in your choice of sauce before serving.

Eggplant Dip with Pita

Ingredients:

- 1 large eggplant
- 2 tbsp tahini
- 2 cloves garlic, minced
- 1 tbsp lemon juice
- Olive oil for drizzling
- Salt and pepper to taste
- Pita bread for serving

Instructions:

Preheat the oven to 400°F (200°C). Prick the eggplant with a fork and roast it whole on a baking sheet for 30-40 minutes until soft. Once cool, scoop out the flesh and combine it with tahini, garlic, lemon juice, salt, and pepper in a food processor. Blend until smooth. Drizzle with olive oil before serving with pita bread.

Brie and Cranberry Tart

Ingredients:

- 1 sheet puff pastry, thawed
- 8 oz brie cheese, sliced
- 1/2 cup cranberry sauce
- Fresh rosemary for garnish
- Egg wash (1 egg beaten with a splash of water)

Instructions:

Preheat the oven to 375°F (190°C). Roll out the puff pastry on a floured surface and cut into a rectangle. Transfer to a baking sheet. Layer the brie slices and cranberry sauce in the center, leaving a border. Fold the edges over the filling and brush with egg wash. Bake for 20-25 minutes until golden brown. Garnish with fresh rosemary.

Shrimp and Grits Bites

Ingredients:

- 1 cup grits
- 2 cups water
- 1 lb shrimp, peeled and deveined
- 2 tbsp butter
- 1/2 cup cheddar cheese, shredded
- Salt and pepper to taste
- Chopped green onions for garnish

Instructions:

Prepare grits by cooking according to package instructions using water. Stir in cheddar cheese, salt, and pepper. Allow to cool slightly, then scoop into small cups or molds. In a skillet, melt butter and cook shrimp until pink and cooked through, about 3-4 minutes. Top grits with shrimp and garnish with green onions.

Parmesan Crisps with Dip

Ingredients:

- 1 cup grated Parmesan cheese
- 1/2 tsp garlic powder
- 1/2 tsp Italian seasoning
- Your choice of dip (salsa, hummus, or ranch)

Instructions:

Preheat the oven to 400°F (200°C). Line a baking sheet with parchment paper. In a bowl, combine Parmesan cheese, garlic powder, and Italian seasoning. Scoop tablespoon-sized amounts onto the baking sheet, flattening them slightly. Bake for 5-7 minutes until golden and crispy. Serve with your choice of dip.

Stuffed Mini Peppers

Ingredients:

- 12 mini bell peppers, halved and seeded
- 1 cup cream cheese, softened
- 1/2 cup cooked sausage or bacon, crumbled
- 1/2 cup shredded cheese (cheddar or mozzarella)
- Salt and pepper to taste

Instructions:

Preheat the oven to 375°F (190°C). In a bowl, mix cream cheese, sausage or bacon, cheese, salt, and pepper. Fill each mini pepper half with the mixture. Arrange on a baking sheet and bake for 15-20 minutes until heated through and bubbly.

Caviar on Blinis

Ingredients:

- 12 blinis (store-bought or homemade)
- 4 oz caviar (fish roe)
- 1/4 cup sour cream
- Fresh dill for garnish

Instructions:

Place blinis on a serving platter. Top each blini with a dollop of sour cream and a spoonful of caviar. Garnish with fresh dill and serve immediately.

Feta and Spinach Stuffed Pastries

Ingredients:

- 1 sheet puff pastry, thawed
- 1 cup fresh spinach, chopped
- 4 oz feta cheese, crumbled
- 1 egg, beaten (for egg wash)
- Salt and pepper to taste

Instructions:

Preheat the oven to 375°F (190°C). In a bowl, combine spinach, feta, salt, and pepper. Roll out the puff pastry and cut into squares. Place a spoonful of the filling in the center of each square, fold over to form a triangle, and seal the edges with a fork. Brush with egg wash and bake for 20-25 minutes until golden.

Garlic Parmesan Cauliflower Bites

Ingredients:

- 1 head cauliflower, cut into florets
- 1/4 cup olive oil
- 1/4 cup grated Parmesan cheese
- 2 cloves garlic, minced
- Salt and pepper to taste

Instructions:

Preheat the oven to 425°F (220°C). In a bowl, toss cauliflower florets with olive oil, Parmesan cheese, garlic, salt, and pepper. Spread on a baking sheet in a single layer and roast for 25-30 minutes until golden and crispy, stirring halfway through. Serve warm.